U.S. Department of Justice
Office of Justice Programs
Office of Juvenile Justice and Delinquency Prevention

J. Robert Flores, Administrator   Juvenile Justice Practices Series

JUVENILE JUSTICE BULLETIN

September 2005

Alternatives to the Secure Detention and Confinement of Juvenile Offenders

James Austin, Kelly Dedel Johnson, and Ronald Weitzer

The Office of Juvenile Justice and Delinquency Prevention (OJJDP) is presenting a Juvenile Justice Practices Series to provide the field with updated research, promising practices, and tools for a variety of juvenile justice areas. These Bulletins are important resources for youth-serving professionals involved in developing and adopting juvenile justice policies and programs, regardless of their funding sources.

This fifth Bulletin in the series promotes reducing the court's reliance on detention and confinement through administrative reforms and special program initiatives informed by an objective assessment of a youth's risk level.

Court officials must balance the interests of public safety with the needs of youth when making decisions about which program to place a juvenile offender and which level of restriction is required. Juvenile offenders who commit serious and/or violent crime may require confinement to protect public safety and intensive supervision and intervention to become rehabilitated. On the other hand, many offenders can be effectively rehabilitated through community-based supervision and intervention.

Secure detention differs from secure confinement both in terms of the reasons a youth is being held and in the range and intensity of programs available to an offender in each setting. Secure detention refers to the holding of youth, upon arrest, in a juvenile detention facility (e.g., juvenile hall) for two main purposes: to ensure the youth appears for all court hearings and to protect the community from future offending. In contrast, secure confinement refers to youth who have been adjudicated delinquent and are committed to the custody of correctional facilities for periods generally ranging from a few months to several years. These confinement facilities have a much broader array of programs than detention facilities.

Status offenders do not require secure detention to ensure their compliance with court orders or to protect public safety. However, recent data indicate that one-third of all youth held in juvenile detention centers are detained for status offenses and technical violations of probation (Arthur, 2001). Detaining youth in facilities prior to adjudication should be an option of last resort only for serious, violent, and chronic offenders and for those who repeatedly fail to appear for scheduled court dates. Secure detention and confinement are almost never appropriate for status offenders and certain other small groups of offenders—those who are very young, vulnerable, first-time offenders; those charged with nonserious offenses; and those with active, involved parents or strong community-based support systems.

It is the large group of offenders who fall in the middle in terms of the seriousness of their crimes that prove challenging to the juvenile justice system. The public's heightened concern about crime and the increased emphasis on juvenile accountability in the past two decades may have further contributed to the juvenile justice system's reliance on secure detention and confinement for most juvenile offenders. Clearly, quality and accessible community-based alternatives must exist to enable the judicious use of expensive detention and confinement programs to meet the needs of both the juvenile offender and the community.

The Need for Alternatives to Secure Detention and Confinement

Alternatives to secure detention and confinement are needed for several reasons, two of which are described below:

♦ **Crowding.** Over the past 15 years, crowded detention and confinement facilities have become more common. Between 1990 and 1999, the number of delinquency cases involving detention increased by 11 percent, or 33,400 cases (Harms, 2003). Over the same time period, the number of adjudicated cases resulting in out-of-home placement (e.g., training schools, camps, ranches, prviate treatment facilities, group homes) increased 24 percent, from 124,900 in 1990 to 155,200 in 1999 (Puzzanchera, 2003). As a result, approximately 39 percent of all juvenile detention and confinement facilities had more residents than available beds (Sickmund, 2002). As the system becomes more crowded, detention staff must learn how to manage continuous admissions and releases and the general lack of stability in such a setting.

Crowding can create dangerous situations in terms of facility management; it also is detrimental to the rehabilitation and treatment of the youth who are confined. In addition to the logistical problems inherent in crowded conditions (e.g., where youth will sleep, how they will be fed, how they will be educated), crowded conditions can also give rise to violence. Youth are more likely to have to be transported to the emergency room as a result of injuries sustained during interpersonal conflicts in crowded facilities (Sickmund, 2002). Youth who are detained for long periods of time usually do not have the opportunity to participate in programming designed to further their educational development (e.g., obtaining a general equivalency diploma). In addition, treatment programs in detention facilities are not designed to address chronic problems (e.g., substance abuse, history of physical or sexual abuse) requiring sustained and intensive interventions. Instead, programming in detention facilities is generally designed to assist youth in adjusting to the correctional environment, ease the transition back to the community upon release, and identify problems needing long-term intervention. Thus, while the youth is in detention, long-term educational and mental health needs are often put on hold. Between 50 and 70 percent of incarcerated youth have a diagnosable mental illness and up to 19 percent may be suicidal, yet timely treatment is difficult to access in crowded facilities (Wasserman, Ko, and McReynolds, 2004; Mears, 2001). In the worst case scenario, crowded facilities lead to increased institutional violence, higher operational costs, and significant vulnerabilities to litigation to improve the conditions of confinement.

♦ **Unproven effectiveness of detention and confinement.** The time a youth spends in secure detention or confinement is not just time away from negative factors that may have influenced his or her behavior. Detaining or confining youth may also widen the gulf between the youth and positive influences such as family and school. Research on traditional confinement in large training schools (i.e., correctional units housing as many as 100 to 500 youth), where a large majority of confined youth are still held in the United States, has found high recidivism rates. As many as 50–70 percent of previously confined youth are rearrested within 1 or 2 years after release (Wiebush et al., 2005; Krisberg, 1997; Winner et al., 1997; Fagan, 1996). Some states have limited the size of these facilities, while others continue to operate 300- and 400-bed training schools. In either configuration, although the long-term nature of a youth's sentence affords a greater opportunity to provide necessary treatment, educational, vocational, and medical services, confinement in these facilities represents a significant separation from the communities to which all youth will return and therefore creates a substantial obstacle in terms of community reentry upon release.

Community-based programs are cost-effective solutions for a large number of delinquent youth. These alternatives to secure detention and confinement are intended to reduce crowding, cut the costs of operating juvenile detention centers, shield offenders from the stigma of institutionalization, help offenders avoid associating with youth who have more serious delinquent histories, and maintain positive ties between the juvenile and his or her family and community.

Between the 1960s and mid-1990s, significant research demonstrated that community-based programs (e.g., intensive supervision, group homes, day reporting centers, probation) were more effective than traditional correctional programs (e.g., training schools) in reducing recidivism and improving community adjustment (see Howell, 1995, for a review of these studies). Even studies with less favorable results showed that community-based programs produced outcomes similar to those of traditional training schools but at significantly reduced costs (Howell, 1995).

Studies conducted on state and local levels also testify to the effectiveness of well-structured, properly implemented, community-based programs as alternatives to secure correctional environments. For example, Massachusetts relies less on holding youth than most other states, turning instead to a network of small, secure programs for serious offenders (generally fewer than 20 youth per facility), complemented by a full continuum of structured community-based programs for the majority of committed youth. These programs allow for a greater connection between the youth and his or her family, school, and other community-based support systems and have shown powerful effects in reducing subsequent involvement in delinquency (Coates, Miller, and Ohlin, 1978; Krisberg, Austin, and Steele, 1989). States can reduce their reliance on secure detention and confinement, choosing instead to place youth in graduated sanctions programs that are responsive to the risks and needs of the delinquent youth.

Expanding the Use of Alternatives to Secure Detention and Confinement Through Systems Change

Strategically matching youth with needed programming requires a cross-system commitment to the objective assessment, classification, and placement of youth. Assessment and classification tools designed for this purpose require buy-in from multiple stakeholders in various youth-serving agencies. New public-public and public-private partnerships need to focus on the common goal of expanding the use of alternatives to detaining or confining youth. Jurisdictions must forge new relationships with program providers and other state agencies to ensure the delivery of a comprehensive continuum of care and to fill gaps in service delivery. Further, integrating new methodologies (e.g., objective classification and risk assessment instruments) into juvenile justice decisionmaking processes will rely on key systems change strategies, especially in the use of data and scientific research to structure those decisions.

Four approaches are used to reduce the reliance on detention and secure confinement and to improve the overall conditions of confinement in secure facilities. These reform or systems change strategies can be categorized as—

♦ Special program initiatives—often funded by federal, state, or local governments or private foundations—that entice jurisdictions to implement new alternative programs.

- New legislation that requires changes in current agency practices.

- Administrative reforms, whereby an agency issues a new procedure designed to process youth in a manner that does not require additional funding or new legislation.

- Litigation that either local interest groups or the federal government initiate to confront gross violations of juvenile offenders' constitutional rights.

Each approach has its own relative strengths and weaknesses in initiating systemic changes that affect the number of youth held in secure facilities.

Special program initiatives are designed to test innovative approaches in a select number of highly motivated jurisdictions. Typically, the jurisdiction must be willing to craft a relatively small pilot program that delivers treatment services to youth who otherwise would be detained or placed in secure confinement. Absent the delivery of intensive treatment services, targeted youth will recidivate in increasing numbers. Jurisdictions implement special program initiatives most often for several reasons, the primary of which is they face little risk of failing on a large scale because the pilot efforts are relatively small. However, many structural problems that limit its ability to effect large-scale change are associated with this strategy. Usually, the amount of available funds is limited, which means that the number of youth who can be diverted from custody is small. Limited funding also means that high-quality and effective treatment services may not be delivered as promised. Further, when the special funds are exhausted, pilot programs are often discontinued. Even if the program proves to be successful, local conditions that provide incentives in one jurisdiction may not be present in others, making it difficult to simply export the model to other jurisdictions.

Legislative reforms are, by nature, more systemic in scope and are less dependent on the use of treatment services as a condition of reform. In this approach, the state legislature—based on a perceived need for change—enacts new laws requiring the juvenile court or juvenile correctional agencies to alter current practices. In recent years, many states have implemented laws requiring youth adjudicated for certain offenses to be held for a specific period of time or to be tried and sentenced as adults—policies that have resulted in the increased use of detention and confinement. However, legislative reforms can also be used to depopulate juvenile correctional facilities and, in certain key areas, legislative reforms could be quite powerful. For instance, many jurisdictions allow adults in pretrial detention to be released on bail. In addition, adults are, by statute, credited for time spent in pretrial detention. Juveniles generally are not afforded these same options or credits, nor do youth generally receive time off for good behavior, which would reduce the length of their confinement after they have been adjudicated and committed to the juvenile correctional system. Legislative reforms regarding these policies could be a powerful tool in effecting a significant change in the reliance on confinement for juvenile offenders.

Similarly, **administrative reforms** are rarely employed to effect reductions in confinement, but they could be extremely productive. Most states grant the juvenile correctional agency the authority to decide when to release youth from secure confinement. Internal policies and criteria based on agency priorities are developed to govern these decisions. The most attractive feature of administrative reforms, unlike the other approaches noted here, is that they do not necessarily require additional funding, staff, or other resources.

Through its Juvenile Detention Alternatives Initiative (JDAI), the Annie E. Casey Foundation has invested significant resources in developing new administrative practices and alternative programs to reduce the use of secure detention.[1] Among the models developed were several administrative practices

---

[1] Read the Foundation's *Pathways to Juvenile Detention Reform* for guidance on planning, executing, promoting, and sustaining juvenile detention reform (Annie E. Casey Foundation, 2000).

that have proved to be quite successful in large jurisdictions struggling with a burgeoning detention population (Annie E. Casey Foundation, 2000). Key reforms included establishing objective screening criteria and risk assessment instruments (like those described below) to limit the use of secure detention to high-risk cases; case processing reforms (e.g., new police referral procedures, 24-hour intake, reduction of attorney continuances, fast-tracking hearings, case expediters, increased automation) to speed caseflow and to ensure that youth are not held in detention unnecessarily; and alternatives to secure detention to reduce facility overcrowding and to lower operating costs.

Litigation-based reforms are the most divisive and protracted means of achieving systems change. They often require both parties to invest in years of expensive investigation and negotiation to reach a settlement. Although consent decrees have been the vehicle for correcting conditions of confinement such as inadequate medical, mental health, and educational services, passage of the Prison Litigation Reform Act (PLRA) of 1995 (Pub. L. No. 104-134) has severely restricted this approach. The PLRA restricts litigation by prisoners and also curtails the involvement of federal courts in the operations of state correctional facilities. In some cases, however, litigation may be the only method to achieve systemic reforms.

This Bulletin discusses in detail the model of integrating administrative reforms and special program initiatives such as those undertaken by the Annie E. Casey Foundation's JDAI. In this model, an objective assessment of risk and a knowledge of programs that have been shown, through rigorous research, to be more effective than others in reducing recidivism and meeting the diverse needs among juvenile offenders should inform the choice among alternative programs. Specifically, two key companion approaches are required: (1) the development of objective, valid, and reliable tools to make placement decisions among these programs; and (2) the expansion of the existing range of program alternatives to ensure that evidence-based programs with varying levels of restrictiveness and types of services are available. Both approaches must coexist and be enhanced and sustained by ongoing training and development of new programs and public and private partnerships.

Objective Classification and Risk Assessment

Research has shown that approximately 54 percent of males and 73 percent of females arrested will have no further contact with the juvenile justice system (Snyder and Sickmund, 1999). Even without juvenile justice programming, most youth will have no further involvement in the system. The critical task is to target only those youth who need intervention services and to match them with the appropriate kinds and levels of programming they need, rather than to serve youth who are unlikely to commit another crime.

In general, "classification" refers to the process of determining at what level of custody an offender should be assigned. "Risk assessment" refers to the process of determining an offender's risk of reoffending, receiving technical violations, failing to appear before the court, or other negative outcomes. Classification and risk assessment play a vital role in determining the number and type of youth best suited for either diversion or release from confinement. Diversion programs have been criticized at times for expanding the use of sanctions for more minor offenses rather than decreasing the overall number of youth in secure settings. Some critics have claimed that diversion programs are often unable to attract the large number of candidates needed to reduce the size and costs of the detained and confined population (Austin and Krisberg, 1982; Austin, 2001).

To guard against these problems, states should consider both the attributes of good risk assessment and classification instruments and how they can be used at different decision points when developing alternatives to detention and confinement. Without objective classification and risk assessment procedures and policies that have been tested to ensure their reliability and validity, it is extremely difficult for even the best-intentioned program to succeed.

The key attributes of objective classification and risk assessment instruments are:

♦ They employ an objective scoring process.

♦ They use items that can be easily and reliably measured, meaning that the results are consistent both across staff and over time as they relate to individual staff members.

♦ They are statistically associated with future criminal behavior, so that the system can accurately identify offenders with different risk levels.

The type of risk one is trying to predict can range from risk of failure to appear to risk of rearrest, to risk of probation or parole failures on technical grounds, to risk of institutional misconduct, to risk of escape. Classifying confined youth according to their propensity to escape or to commit violent or other serious acts while incarcerated is desirable. However, because these events are quite rare, it is often difficult to develop a predictive instrument. Types of risk vary—so, too, the criteria used to assess risk should vary. Therefore, more than one risk assessment instrument should be used, although they may share many common features.

At times, the level of risk an offender presents becomes secondary to policy objectives and facility priorities. For example, an administrator might want to ensure that certain types of youth are not placed in a low-security setting regardless of their risk of escaping or committing violent crimes (e.g., sex offenders, high-profile inmates). In these situations, the classification system minimizes the potential for a highly publicized negative incident to maintain the integrity of the facility and correctional agency.

Some states have yet to implement any form of objective classification system, some use an objective process at each decision point throughout the system, and some use objective classification instruments to guide certain decisions but not others. When thinking about which type of instrument to use, states should consider how different types of classification and risk assessment systems are appropriate for different decision points in the juvenile justice process (see figure). Key points include the initial detention decision, the decision to use dispositional alternatives (which may include commitment to a secure facility), initial classification, internal classification, and reclassification. At each decision point, an assessment instrument is needed to categorize offenders into the relevant categories, which depend on the objective at each point.

Research and evaluations have shown objective classification and risk assessment systems to be both reliable and valid. The systems ensure that detained and confined youth are assigned to the most appropriate program considering public safety and their needs while permitting them to maintain close relationships with their families and communities when possible. If a youth is assigned to a secure facility, classification and risk assessment procedures help those in authority decide where the youth will be housed, with whom, and to which programs or services he or she will be assigned. Finally, as the youth nears release, classification and risk assessment tools should help staff to determine when and how the youth will be returned to his or her family and community.

Classifying youth should not be arbitrary. To ensure that offenders are classified systematically according to risk level and program needs, specially designated classification staff must be given the authority to transfer and place youth. By understanding the attributes of the confined youth population and combining this knowledge with accurate population projections, juvenile correctional agencies can better estimate their future facility, staffing, and program needs, thereby structuring the facilities to meet the needs of confined youth.

Risk Assessment and Classification at Various Decision Points

Youth enters the system.	**Detention Decision** • Straight release. • Day/evening reporting center. • Supervised release. • Electronic monitoring. • Home detention.
Youth is adjudicated.	**Dispositional Alternatives** • Probation. • Day/evening reporting center. • Residential placement. • Secure confinement.
Youth is committed to a secure facility.	**Initial Classification** • Custody assessment. • Program needs assessment. • Facility designation.
Youth is transferred to an appropriate facility.	**Internal Classification** • Housing assignment. • Program assignment.
Youth is transferred to a designated housing unit.	**Reclassification** • Custody classification. • Internal classification (facility, housing, and programming; community programming).

The Process

Detention risk assessment. After arrest, the first major decision is whether the youth should be detained. In most jurisdictions, the court makes this decision; in others, probation or detention agencies are authorized to determine whether detention is warranted. The initial decision is often reviewed and finalized in a formal detention hearing conducted shortly after a youth's admission to a detention facility (i.e., within 72 hours). If a judge determines that continued detention is required, the youth remains in juvenile hall pending his or her adjudication and disposition. In general, most youth are detained for only a few days and the courts efficiently dispose of their cases. However, youth with more complicated or serious offenses, or those who are awaiting transfer to a commitment program, often remain in detention for weeks or months. When youth languish in detention facilities for a long period, they usually do not have access to the treatment, education, and vocational services that they need.

Much like a pretrial release process in the adult system, an objective detention risk assessment system is needed for juvenile courts and correctional agencies to determine whether youth should be placed in secure confinement while awaiting adjudication and disposition hearings. The two major concerns in reaching such a decision are whether the youth will appear for court hearings and whether the youth is likely to commit additional crimes if released from custody. Such risks should be assessed through objective, valid, and reliable means. Secure detention can then be used sparingly.

The factors to be considered in objective detention risk assessments (and in other classification and risk assessment instruments) can be separated into four categories[2]:

♦ Number and severity of the current charges.

♦ Earlier arrest and juvenile court records.

♦ History of success or failure while under community supervision (e.g., preadjudication, probation, parole).

♦ Other "stability" factors associated with court appearances and reoffending (e.g., age, school attendance, education level, drug/alcohol use, family structure).

Typically, jurisdictions construct an additive point scale to quantify the level of risk that each youth reviewed for release or detention presents to help decisionmakers ensure that low-risk youth charged with nonserious crimes are not placed in detention. Conversely, such instruments also serve to ensure that youth who pose a serious risk to themselves and others are not readily released without proper supervision.

A number of jurisdictions use objective detention risk assessments to reduce the number of youth detained prior to formal adjudication. Sacramento, CA; Multnomah County, OR; and Cook County, IL implemented risk assessment instruments as part of their involvement with the Annie E. Casey Foundation's JDAI. Administrators in Cook County, IL, for example, combined the use of a validated risk assessment instrument with an array of alternatives to detention for those youth who do not require secure custody. Immediately upon a youth's arrest, on-call probation staff complete an objective detention risk assessment before the initial detention decision. The assessment's numerical score produces a recommendation to either detain or release and, if release is recommended, the assessment outlines any special conditions that may be required.

---

[2] These categories have been shown to have statistically significant relationships to recidivism among juvenile offenders (see, e.g., Johnson, Wagner, and Matthews, 2002; Hardyman, 1999).

These new programs and procedures ensured that law enforcement had additional options for dealing with delinquent youth. The implementation of this detention risk assessment system in the 1990s, which was part of the county's larger effort to reduce crowding in its detention facilities, resulted in the effective diversion of many youth who previously would have been detained (Lubow, 1999). The number of annual admissions to the Cook County detention center was reduced by approximately 1,100 cases between 1995 and 1997, with the rate of admission for detention referrals decreasing from 70 percent to approximately 45 percent (Stanfield, 2000). A copy of Cook County's Detention Risk Screening Instrument is presented in appendix A.

A similar effort is now underway in Georgia where a comprehensive detention risk assessment system has been implemented as part of a memorandum of agreement between the state and the U.S. Department of Justice (resulting from a Civil Rights of Institutionalized Persons Act investigation). Preliminary results indicate that the system has not had as much impact on the detention system's crowded conditions as originally hoped. In contrast to Cook County, which significantly decreased crowding after recalibrating some of the items and category weights[3] (Stanfield, 2000), Georgia has not, to date, experienced those same decreases due to lack of complete buy-in from all stakeholders. Whereas a pilot test of the instrument showed it to be both valid and reliable, the state's sporadic use of the instrument in all jurisdictions has limited its effectiveness. A copy of the instrument is provided in appendix B.

Risk assessment to guide court dispositional alternatives. The juvenile court has wide discretion over who shall be committed to confinement and, in certain cases, the length of that sentence. Unlike the structured guidelines that the adult system has adopted, few jurisdictions have attempted to develop a structured mechanism to guide juvenile placement decisions among an array of dispositional alternatives. This is not surprising because most states have retained an indeterminate sentencing structure without guidelines. Nonetheless, states should, at a minimum, examine regularly the level of disparity in sentencing that may occur within their juvenile courts and try to minimize any differences through training and legislative reform. Systems change efforts may be required to leverage the power of both laws and policies to ensure sentencing decisions are free from bias and inconsistency.

States that decide to develop placement guidelines for the juvenile court should base them on both policy considerations and empirical research. Using a consensus-building process, representatives from a cross-section of juvenile justice decisionmakers determine the items to be included, their relative weights, the severity ranking of current offenses, and which types of placement will be available to different types of offenders. Once validated, scores representing the risk to reoffend can be combined with a matrix identifying various placement options. Using such instruments, the court can suggest community-based alternatives for offenders with lower scores, while offenders with higher scores are considered for secure custody.

Wiebush and colleagues (1995) highlight the benefits of the matrix approach—most importantly, that the two dimensions of risk and proportionality are derived separately (the former, empirically, and the latter, from a consensus-based process). This separation permits decisionmakers to make distinctions among youth who commit similar offenses but who differ in their risk to reoffend. Two examples of placement instruments are presented in appendixes C and D.

External/custody classification. If a youth is assigned to secure confinement, staff should apply a specific classification instrument to establish custody level, thereby determining the type of facility to which the youth should be assigned. Some youth may require long-term placement in a maximum security facility, while others may be better suited to a short-term program with fewer security

---

[3] Cook County changed the wording on some items and increased or decreased the number of points awarded for various items to ensure that scores on the instrument were statistically associated with risk.

restrictions. These decisions should be based on the seriousness of the youth's current offense, prior system involvement, history of escape, and other factors shown to be related to the risk posed to public safety. In the detention risk assessment process, youth are sometimes placed in restrictive settings regardless of their level of risk because agency policy or state law requires it. The custody classification system strives to place the youth in the least restrictive custody level required to ensure the safety of staff and other youth.

Custody classification has four essential components—initial screening, initial classification, reclassification, and program needs assessment:

♦ **Initial screening.** Trained intake staff should screen youth immediately after their assignment to secure confinement. The most common type of screening instrument is a checklist with questions regarding the youth's medical and mental health needs, substance abuse history, and other information that might indicate the need to place the youth in a special housing unit for further assessment and observation by medical, mental health, and classification staff. The major objective of this review is to ensure that youth with severe mental health, medical, and other management issues are identified so they can be separated from the general confinement population until a more careful assessment can been made.

   Initial screening is also important for detention facilities. As indicated earlier, the high volume of admissions and the relatively short length of stays reflect a detained population that is in constant flux. Because many youth only spend a few days in detention, often there is not enough time to secure all of the public records required for a rigorous classification assessment.

♦ **Initial classification.** Classification staff determine a youth's custody level using an initial classification form that includes standard risk factors for escape or institutional misconduct. Because many youth are experiencing their first admission to a custodial setting, initial classification places emphasis on the youth's current offense, prior juvenile record, success or failure on probation, and various measures of community stability (e.g., age, school attendance, family structure). If the youth has been confined previously, his or her earlier institutional conduct should also play an important role in the initial assessment. A copy of Georgia's initial classification form is provided in appendix E.

♦ **Reclassification.** The reclassification form is used to reassess the youth's initial classification designation through a review of his or her conduct during the first 60 to 90 days in a facility. Consequently, it places more emphasis on institutional behavior and less on the youth's prior offenses and criminal history. Youth with the longest period of confinement will occupy the greatest proportion of a facility's bed capacity and are most likely to be reclassified on a regular basis. Because most youth will not become involved in serious misconduct, the reclassification process allows youth with positive behavior patterns to be placed in lower custody levels and thus will conserve expensive high-security bedspace. A copy of Georgia's custody reclassification form is provided in appendix F.

♦ **Program needs assessment.** The final component of a custody classification system requires that each youth's need for services and treatment be assessed in a more indepth manner than during the initial screening.[4] The resulting data are used to assign a youth to a facility, housing unit, or program that provides the most appropriate and most needed services commensurate with the youth's custody level. For example, if a needs assessment reveals a youth's heavy involvement with alcohol and/or drugs, his or her placement in a residential substance abuse treatment housing wing or program would be appropriate. Staff with expertise in mental health, education, vocational training, and medical care

---

[4] The needs assessment looks for issues requiring long-term treatment, whereas the initial screening typically looks for issues that would put the youth in immediate danger (e.g., suicidal behavior, medical conditions).

should conduct the needs assessment process. In some systems, separate assessments are required to learn if the youth is eligible for special education services, has mental health disorders, or has other special needs that staff without specialized training may not have detected. Specialized assessments need to be reviewed and consolidated into a single comprehensive treatment plan under the direction of a caseworker or treatment committee.

Internal classification. After the youth is assigned to a facility through external classification, internal classification should be used to determine where the youth will be housed and in which programs he or she will participate. The housing decision is critical, as many incidents that require staff to use force often stem from either an improper housing decision or lack of proper supervision. Most juvenile correctional facilities have self-contained housing units with one or more youth to a room and open areas in which large numbers of youth congregate to watch television, play card games, and engage in other recreational activities. It is in these environments that internal classification systems play a critical role. If implemented properly, the number of adverse incidents can be reduced.

In making internal classification decisions, a number of factors should be considered. For example, physical size, history of mental illness, medical condition, and gang involvement are reasons to either separate certain youth from one another or house them in specialized units. It may also be useful to create special housing units that reward youth for good institutional conduct. A copy of Georgia's internal classification form/housing matrix are provided in appendix G.

Parole/community release and reentry. The last critical decision point to be governed by objective classification is the decision to release a youth from custody. This decision has gained greater attention on a national level under the rubric of "reentry" or "offender transition." In some states (e.g., California, Illinois), a juvenile parole board makes the decision; in others, it is the judge's decision. Elsewhere, the juvenile correctional agency has broad discretion about whom to release and when. The agency's ranking of offense severity and risk of recidivism often governs this decision. The release decision is very similar to the detention risk assessment decision, as both are primarily concerned with risk to public safety.

A number of jurisdictions use the same instrument to determine the level of community supervision that probationers and parolees need, typically modeled after the Model Case Management System (Baird, Sturrs, and Connelly, 1984; Wiebush et al., 1995). Using a set of eight items shown to have a statistical relationship to the likelihood of reoffending, the instrument distinguishes groups of offenders with different levels of risk, suggesting that different levels of community supervision are needed. A template for such an instrument is presented in appendix H.

Common Attributes of Classification and Risk Assessment Systems

The foundation of systems change relies on data and accountability. Criminal justice data are used, for example, in estimating the need for specific services among the at-risk population, projecting the number of eligible participants for a new program or service, and identifying an intervention's effectiveness in reducing recidivism or attaining other long-term outcomes. Nowhere, however, is the need to rely on data more critical than in the development of objective classification and risk assessment instruments. Although common sense and professional experience may certainly guide the initial construction of the tools, the individual items and the weights used in scoring must be found to be statistically related to the targeted outcome (e.g., risk of failure to appear, risk to reoffend). Further, solid data and statistical relationships are at the heart of developing training modules to ensure the proper use of the instruments. Ensuring that two staff would classify a given youth in the same way and ensuring the integrity of override provisions are particularly critical.

Objective classification and risk assessment systems must allow for some level of discretion through the use of overrides. Any classification or risk assessment system will produce a substantial number of false positives (offenders who were predicted to recidivate but do not) and false negatives (offenders who were expected to succeed but do not). Consequently, staff must have the ability to alter, or override, the scored custody level based on their professional judgment and consideration of other factors that may not be related to risk. The danger is that overrides, if used excessively, can easily undermine consistent decisionmaking. Conversely, if overrides are underused, staff may not be exercising the appropriate level of professional judgment, which also serves to misclassify youth.

The general standard is that 5 to 15 percent of the confined population should be classified based on an override and not the original classification score. Furthermore, override decisions should be balanced: half of the overrides should result in a lower custody or risk level and half should result in a higher custody or risk level.

Override factors should be separated into two types—discretionary and nondiscretionary. The former reflects a decision by the classification staff to depart from the scored custody level. For example, if a youth is scored as minimum custody but the staff believes that he or she poses a higher risk to the security of the facility's operations, the scored custody level can be overridden to medium custody. However, a supervisor must review and approve such overrides to ensure staff are using them in an appropriate manner.

Nondiscretionary overrides, as their name implies, are mandatory and must be used in certain situations. For example, the agency may have a policy that all youth tried as adults or who will be transferred to the adult correctional system after reaching age 18 will never be classified lower than medium custody. Similarly, a jurisdiction may have a policy that youth adjudicated for serious sex offenses may not be placed in minimum custody until they are within 60 days of their scheduled release dates.

Objective classification and risk assessment systems are important tools for ensuring that youth are placed in assignments that provide a level of supervision commensurate with the level of risk that the youth presents. Many youth can do well under community supervision or in community-based programs that avoid the negative consequences of secure custody (e.g., high program costs, separation from family and community). The key is selecting the youth who are appropriate for these alternative programs without jeopardizing public safety. Objective instruments, such as those described above, can provide a systematic method for placement in alternative programs and can guide the sensible use of expensive, secure-custody beds.

Special Program Initiatives

The second resource needed to decrease reliance on secure custody is an array of alternative programs that feature varying levels of supervision and types of services. In FY 2000, 16 states and territories used OJJDP funds to reduce their reliance on secure custody. Of these, seven states had done so from 1995 to 2000. Funded program activities included victim and offender mediation and rehabilitation, workshops, peer courts, electronic monitoring, and home detention. Unfortunately, very few of these programs have conducted rigorous evaluations to measure their effectiveness.

However, rigorous evaluation of a number of other programs that provide alternatives to secure custody have been shown to be effective. Because relatively few studies have been done on any one type of program, replication evaluations of comparable programs in different jurisdictions are clearly needed. In many cases, evaluation studies of a particular program type differ in the research methods and juvenile samples used (Lipsey and Wilson, 1998), making it difficult to compare results across sites even within the same program category. Finally, some programs have been evaluated soon after implementation. Such evaluations must be treated with caution because, typically, some time after initial implementation is needed for a program to become fully institutionalized and to produce consistent results. As Lipsey and Wilson (1998) noted, programs more than 2 years old tend to produce larger positive effects on their clientele than newer programs.

Examples of Alternatives to Secure Detention

Several alternatives to secure detention are outlined here—from outright release to supervised release to residential programs.

Outright release. Few published studies have examined directly or indirectly the effectiveness of releasing youth to their families prior to adjudication. A study from Kentucky reported that when court personnel strictly adhered to criteria for detaining youth, the number of youth released to their families or nonsecure residential alternatives was substantially increased. The result was a slight increase in the number of failures to appear before the court but no increase in rearrests prior to final case disposition (Kihm and Block, 1982).

Supervised release. Youth judged too risky for outright release, either because they are unlikely to appear for adjudication or are likely to commit new offenses, can be placed on supervised release rather than in secure detention. Federal mandates to reduce the number of youth held in secure detention have fostered the development of various enhanced supervision programs aimed at youth considered too risky for traditional unsupervised release. The programs discussed below—home detention, electronic monitoring, intensive supervision, day and evening reporting centers, and skills training programs— provide more intensive supervision than ordinary probation, and many also provide services to help troubled youth and their families.

♦ **Home detention.** In contrast to outright release, home detention requires offenders to remain at home during specified time periods: (1) at all times, (2) at all times except when in school or working, or (3) at night (curfews). Additional conditions such as drug testing may also be imposed. Youth who violate these conditions risk being placed in secure detention. Home detention programs vary in the intensity of contact between supervisors and youth, but contacts are more frequent (often daily) than in the case of traditional probation. Many, but not all, home detention programs use paraprofessional outreach workers in lieu of probation officers to both mentor and supervise youth. Home detention provides considerable cost savings compared with secure and nonsecure placements (Ball, Huff, and Lilly, 1988).

Descriptive studies report high levels of success: most youth appear for adjudication and only a small proportion are returned to detention for new offenses. An evaluation of a program in Tuscaloosa County, AL, found that home detainees were no more likely to recidivate than a preadjudicatory group held in secure detention (Smykla and Selke, 1982). A study of seven different home detention programs, six of which provided counseling or other services in addition to supervision, found that most youth (71–89 percent) completed the programs without incident and appeared in court (Young and Pappenfort, 1979). Between 8 percent and 25 percent of the youth were returned to secure detention, mostly for violations of their conditions of release but very few (2–5 percent) for committing new offenses. In Ohio, 91 percent of youth detained at home did not reoffend, appearing in court for adjudication. A San Diego program reported a 97-percent success rate for home detention clients (Ball, Huff, and Lilly, 1988).

♦ **Electronic monitoring.** Electronic monitoring, often used in conjunction with home detention, monitors an offender's whereabouts via an electronic device attached to the wrist or ankle and by random phone calls to his or her residence. Electronic monitoring is intended to reduce the costs of supervision, reduce institutional populations, allow the offender to remain in school while under supervision, and enhance the potential for rehabilitation by keeping offenders at home and in close contact with family members. Few published evaluations of electronic monitoring exist, even though such monitoring is widely used for juveniles (Cohn et al., 1997; Torbet, 1999). Some evidence does show that youth differ from adults in their response to electronic monitoring (Roy, 1997). Vaughn (1989) reviewed eight electronic monitoring programs. Most were used as alternatives to prehearing detention, four were used to supplement probation, and three were used for offenders released early from an institution. Failure rates in the programs ranged from 4.5 percent to 30 percent; most of the failures resulted from technical violations rather than new offenses. A study of youth detained at home in Lake County, IN, reported that those assigned to electronic monitoring had a higher program completion rate (90 percent versus 75 percent) and a lower recidivism rate (17 percent versus 26 percent) than youth who were not monitored electronically (Roy and Brown, 1995).

◆ **Intensive supervision.** Many intensive supervision programs (ISPs) function primarily as alternatives to confinement for adjudicated offenders (to be discussed later). But ISPs can also serve as alternatives to secure detention for juvenile arrestees. One model program is San Francisco's Detention Diversion Advocacy Program (DDAP), an ISP that incorporates rehabilitative treatments tailored to offenders' special needs. Parents, the public defender's office, the probation department, and community agencies refer juveniles to DDAP. Among the referred youth, DDAP identifies those likely to be detained prior to adjudication, designs a release plan that includes a list of community services and specific objectives that DDAP will oversee, and presents this plan to the court. Offenders live at home or at a suitable alternative site in the community and meet with DDAP case managers a minimum of three times a week. Offenders' families are also provided with needed services.

An evaluation study that the Youth Guidance Center conducted in 1997 compared 271 DDAP clients with a random sample of 271 youth who spent at least 3 days in detention (Sheldon, 1999). Using various measures of recidivism and controlling for age, risk score, number of prior referrals, number of previous out-of-home placements, nature of prior offenses, and race, the center found that the DDAP group was significantly less likely to recidivate than the detained group. The overall recidivism rate for the DDAP group was about half that for the detained group (34 percent versus 60 percent, respectively). Similarly large differences were found in recidivism involving violent crimes. DDAP success rates are even more striking because the DDAP group had a greater percentage of high-risk youth than the control group.

Sheldon (1999) suggests a number of reasons for DDAP's success: small caseloads, caseworkers' freedom from bureaucratic restrictions of the juvenile justice system, the similar backgrounds of DDAP caseworkers and clients, and an emphasis on rehabilitative services coupled with specific goals to track clients' progress. Any assessment of the program must consider that DDAP personnel selected DDAP clients, raising the possibility of selection effects on the outcome. DDAP case managers may have selected clients who were most likely to succeed in the program. It is thus difficult to determine how much of the program's remarkable success is due to the clients selected or to the program itself, but if the positive results were largely due to the program, this would appear to be a model worth replicating elsewhere. Further details on the program are available in the OJJDP Bulletin, *Detention Diversion Advocacy: An Evaluation* (Sheldon, 1999).

For additional information, contact:

Center on Juvenile and Criminal Justice
54 Dore Street
San Francisco, CA 94103
415–621–5661

415–621–5466 (fax)
or
1234 Massachusetts Avenue NW., Suite C1009
Washington, DC 20005
202–737–7270
202–737–7271 (fax)
cjcj@cjcj.org
www.cjcj.org

♦ **Day and evening reporting centers.** Day and evening reporting centers are nonresidential programs that require offenders to report daily activities to case managers. They are a mechanism for enhanced supervision of offenders but differ from ISPs because they provide services such as drug treatment, job training referrals, life skills services, and counseling. Little research exists on juvenile reporting centers.

One promising program model for juveniles is found in Cook County, IL, where minors charged with a probation violation or apprehended on a warrant participate 5 nights a week in county-funded evening reporting center programs. The goal of these programs is to prevent prehearing detention—the focus is exclusively on preventing delinquent behavior and ensuring that youth appear in court. Evening reporting centers operate from 4 p.m. to 9 p.m. daily, and participants are involved with the program for between 5 and 21 days (generally, until their next court date). Youth participate in educational and vocational programs, counseling, recreational activities, and life development workshops (e.g., lectures on delinquency, local government, alcohol and drugs, and health issues; workshops on conflict resolution, employment, and parenting skills). Dinner is provided as an incentive for participation. Center staff work closely with home confinement officers and probation staff to transport youth to and from the program. Seven facilities currently handle about 25 youth each; the newest center targets families. The program evidenced a success rate of 92 percent from December 1995 to August 2001. Youth were determined to be successful if they were not rearrested while participating in the program. The average length of participation for successful youth was 21 calendar days. As of August 2001, Cook County's evening reporting centers have served 7,730 youth.

For additional information, contact:

Mark Morrissey, Deputy Chief Probation Officer
Juvenile Probation and Court Services
Circuit Court of Cook County
1100 South Hamilton Avenue
Chicago, IL 60612
312–433–6569
www.cookcountycourt.org/services

♦ **Skills training programs.** One example of a nonresidential skills training program is Fresh Start, Baltimore, MD. Fresh Start was established to provide hands-on training and education for juvenile delinquents in the Baltimore area. The primarily voluntary program targets youth ages 16–19 who are convicted of nonviolent crimes and who typically come from low-income, high-crime neighborhoods. The 40-week program is designed to help youth learn practical skills such as carpentry and boat repair and to integrate education and employment experience. Fresh Start has recently partnered with local colleges so that program graduates can attend college-level courses at a reduced cost. In 2000, Fresh Start added a Workforce Development Center to its array of program services. Each Fresh Start graduate is assigned to a job retention counselor who helps the youth navigate common workplace challenges. Approximately 90 males graduate from the program each year. Approximately 50 percent of those who enter the program complete all modules, and those who finish the first 8 weeks have an 80-percent completion rate. Fresh Start tracks its graduates for 3 years after program completion. Graduates from 1997 to 2000 had a rearrest rate of 19 percent and a reincarceration rate of 7 percent, well below the rearrest rate of 75 percent that other Maryland Department of Juvenile Justice programs reported.[5] About 66 percent of the graduates were employed, and 15 percent continued their education (figures provided by Fresh Start). Currently, another Fresh Start program is being established in Washington, DC. Seventy percent of the funding comes from a contract with the Maryland Department of Juvenile Justice, and the remainder comes from philanthropic and corporate donations.

For additional information, contact:

Greg Rapisarda
Fresh Start
Living Classrooms Foundation
802 South Caroline Street
Baltimore, MD 21231
410–685–0295
202–479–6710, ext. 240
410–752–8433 (fax)
www.livingclassrooms.org

Residential programs. Not all youth can reasonably or safely be returned to their homes, but neither do they warrant secure detention. Residential programs for youth awaiting adjudication are less studied than at-home alternatives. Young and Pappenfort (1979) analyzed foster home programs, detention homes, and programs for runaways that serve as alternatives to secure detention. Youth in these programs had negligible rates of new offenses while awaiting adjudication and low rates (10 percent or less) of running away. Many jurisdictions administer combinations of residential programs and various at-home alternatives. Lubow (1999) evaluated three JDAI programs that the Casey Foundation sponsored in Cook County, IL; Multnomah County, OR; and Sacramento County, CA. The programs combined home confinement, day or evening reporting centers, and temporary, nonsecure shelters. In all three sites, the alternative programs were implemented without sacrificing appearance-in-court rates or pretrial rearrest rates. In Cook County, for example, the failure-to-appear rate was reduced by 50 percent (Lubow, 1999). More recent data on the Cook County programs for youth served between January 1997 and August 2001 indicate the completion rate[6] for program participants was 93 percent for home confinement, 92 percent for evening reporting centers, 94 percent for electronic monitoring, and 96 percent for nonsecure shelters (figures provided by Cook County Circuit Court).

---

[5] See PEPNet's Web site.
[6] Remaining free of arrest while in the program, not after release.

For additional information, contact:

Mark Morrissey, Deputy Chief Probation Officer
Juvenile Probation and Court Services
Circuit Court of Cook County
1100 South Hamilton Avenue
Chicago, IL 60612
312–433–6569
www.cookcountycourt.org

An example of a residential skills program that is not combined with an at-home alternative is the Gulf Coast Trades Center (GCTC), a private, nonprofit organization that has served troubled youth in the Houston, TX, area since 1971. GCTC serves youth ages 16–19 who are referred by the Texas Youth Commission or by a probation officer. The program provides education, job training, life skills planning, and aftercare programs. GCTC also runs the Youth Industry Program, which trains youth in carpentry skills, and the Raven School, which prepares students to take the General Educational Development test. Other youth are trained and permitted to work in the culinary arts, horticulture, automotive technology, desktop publishing, and secretarial positions. Recent evaluation results demonstrate that from September 1999 through August 2000, 84 percent of the participating youth completed the program and 70 percent were employed when they left the program. In addition, 1999–2000 graduates had a 16-percent rearrest rate, compared with a rearrest rate of approximately 54 percent among all youth released from the Texas Youth Commission in 1999.[7]

For additional information, contact:

Thomas Buzbee
Gulf Coast Trades Center
143 Forest Service Road, #233
New Waverly, TX 77358
936–344–6677
936–344–2386 (fax)
gctc@gctcw.org
www.gctcw.org

Examples of Alternatives to Secure Confinement

In the 1970s and 1980s, alternative programs for juveniles targeted status offenders and less serious delinquents. Since then, an increasing number of programs, including intensive supervision and home detention, serve more serious offenders along with status offenders and minor delinquents. Other programs, such as group homes, are specifically designed to accommodate the needs and risks of chronic or serious and violent offenders outside the walls of traditional correctional facilities.

Diversion. Diversion takes place when law enforcement and court personnel exercise their discretion to keep individual youth from entering the court's jurisdiction. This has long been an integral, and largely unstudied, part of the juvenile justice system. Diversion programs began to appear in the 1970s in response to concerns regarding deteriorating conditions in crowded juvenile institutions, federal mandates and funding, and legal action by youth advocates. Diversion programs divert youth from traditional forms of secure detention and confinement into a variety of alternative treatments and modes of supervision.

---

[7] Figures provided by GCTC and found on the Texas Youth Commission's Web site.

Generally, youth in diversion programs are not wholly removed from the jurisdiction of the juvenile court and its traditional sanctioning powers.

Empirical studies of diversion conducted in the 1970s yielded mixed results: some studies found that recidivism was reduced, others found no positive effects on recidivism, and still others yielded mixed results (Stanford, 1984; Ezell, 1992). More recent studies of diversion (Rojek, 1986; Davidson et al., 1990) have found significant effects in reducing recidivism. More compelling evidence of the efficacy of diversion is found when a diversionary philosophy is embraced on a statewide basis. In 1974, Massachusetts closed its training schools and developed a range of alternative community-based programs and small-scale secure facilities. An initial analysis of statewide data did not indicate lower recidivism rates for community-based clients than for training school offenders, but in areas of Massachusetts where community-based programs were implemented properly, with a diversity of programs available, recidivism among the youth in community-based programs decreased (Coates, Miller, and Ohlin, 1978). A later study of the Massachusetts system found that recidivism rates in the state were better than or equal to those in other states studied (Krisberg, Austin, and Steele, 1989). Utah closely replicated the Massachusetts example and, after the first year, experienced a significant decline in recidivism among serious and chronic juvenile offenders (Krisberg and Howell, 1998). The example of Massachusetts suggests that "what works" may not be any one particular alternative program but rather a variety of programs that can be drawn on to meet the different needs of a diverse population of juvenile offenders and their communities.

Intensive supervision programs. ISPs are sometimes only nominally intensive. Some differ very little from traditional supervision, with intermittent contacts and surveillance. Some studies of ISPs find little difference in recidivism rates compared with either traditional probation or confinement (Greenwood and Turner, 1993; Murray and Cox, 1979), while other studies report lower recidivism rates for program youth or recidivism rates comparable to youth released from confinement, often at a lower cost (Barton and Butts, 1990; Fratto and Hallstrom, 1978; Wiebush, 1993).

Sontheimer and Goodstein (1993) found that intensive supervision and aftercare paid off for serious juvenile offenders in Pennsylvania in that they were less likely to reoffend than offenders who received traditional probation. Studying a North Carolina project, Land and colleagues (1990) found that intensive supervision and aftercare reduced future offending more significantly among youth who committed less serious offenses—primarily status offenses (e.g., running away, truancy)—than did traditional supervision. In addition to concerns about the appropriateness of placing status offenders in an intensive supervision program, after 3½ years, researchers also found no long-term difference in subsequent delinquency between youth assigned to intensive supervision and those assigned to traditional supervision (Land, McCall, and Parker, 1994). Whether an ISP is linked to appropriate rehabilitation services or is based simply on monitoring and control seems to influence an ISP's chances of success (MacKenzie, 1997).

Several demonstration ISPs exist, including those in Wayne County, MI, and Lucas County, OH. Barton and Butts (1990) conducted a 5-year evaluation of three home-based ISPs in Wayne County, comparing juveniles randomly assigned to the home-based programs with similar groups of youth committed to state institutions. Recidivism rates, measured using official charges and self-report data, were comparable for experimental and control group youth. The latter were more likely to be charged with serious offenses and less likely to be charged with status offenses than the former. The controls were also likely to reoffend more quickly after release than the youth assigned to an ISP.

Wiebush (1993) conducted a similar study in Lucas County, OH. This ISP involved small caseloads, frequent contacts with offenders, mandatory community service, involvement in treatment services, and control measures such as random drug tests and curfews. Wiebush compared youth in an ISP with those paroled after release from a Department of Youth Services (DYS) facility. Both groups registered fairly high recidivism rates within 18 months of release—82 percent for the ISP youth and 83 percent for the DYS youth. No significant differences existed between the groups in rates for felony, misdemeanor, or status offense charges, but the ISP youth were significantly more likely to be charged with technical violations of probation/parole.

An example of a successful intensive probation program that includes a wide range of services and programs for youth and their families is the Tarrant County Advocate Program-North (TCAP) in Texas. Started in November 1994, TCAP is funded by Tarrant County Juvenile Services. Approximately 50 youth at a time participate in the 4–6-month program, which serves an average of 210 youth per year. Most are male (95 percent) and Hispanic (49 percent) or white (47 percent), and approximately 80 percent are involved with gangs. TCAP uses paid mentors or advocates to link youth and their families with community-based services. These advocates contact the families three or four times per week, tailoring the program to fit individual family needs. Program activities include counseling, job training, subsidized youth employment, vocational training, anger management classes, tutoring, community service restitution projects, character development courses, and parent education classes. During 2002, TCAP served 527 youth and their families; 385 families completed the program. Of these youth, 96 percent were successfully maintained in the community or were diverted from out-of-home placement or commitment to the Texas Youth Commission.[8]

For additional information, contact:

Belinda Hampton, Director
Tarrant County Advocate Program-North
112 NW. 24th Street, Suite 118
Fort Worth, TX 76106
817–625–4185
817–625–4187 (fax)

Community-based treatment and therapy. Multisystemic therapy (MST) has been introduced in at least 25 locations in the United States and Canada. As of 1998, more than $10 million has been spent researching its effectiveness. Designed to address multiple factors linked to juvenile antisocial and illegal behaviors, MST may be appropriate for youth with serious behavior disorders, including violent and chronic offenders who might otherwise be confined. MST youth remain at home and receive treatment focused on their interpersonal, peer, family, and school problems and needs. One goal is to promote parental supervision and authority. A review of research evaluating MST programs in a number of southern states showed decreased rates of recidivism among violent and chronic juvenile offenders (Henggeler, 1997). Available literature suggests that MST is one of the most effective treatments (Lipsey and Wilson, 1998; Krisberg and Howell, 1998; Cullen and Gendreau, 2000).

Studies of violent and chronic juvenile offenders find that MST programs register between 25- and 70-percent reductions in rates of rearrest and are also linked to decreases in youth's mental health problems and improvements in family functioning (Mihalic et al., 2001). MST has been evaluated in multiple well-designed clinical trials (Henggeler et al., 1998; Kazdin and Weisz, 1998; Thorton et al., 2000). These studies, conducted in Memphis, TN, and South Carolina, show that MST participation can have significant positive effects on juvenile offenders' problem behavior (including conduct problems, anxiety withdrawal, immaturity, and socialized aggression), family relations, and self-reported offenses immediately after treatment. Fifty-nine weeks after referral, MST youth had slightly more than half as many new arrests than control group youth, spent an average of 73 fewer days incarcerated in juvenile

---

[8] See Tarrant County's Web site.

justice facilities, and showed reductions in aggression with peers. After nearly 2½ years, MST youth were half as likely to be rearrested as control group youth.

One promising MST program is the Family and Neighborhood Services (FANS) project in South Carolina. Operating out of a community mental health center, the project is based on the principle that multiple types of interventions (family, community, school, etc.) are needed for juvenile offenders. FANS assigned small caseloads to therapists who worked with juveniles and their families for an average of 4 months. Caseworkers had frequent, often daily, contact with these families. Juveniles in the program had substantial offense histories, averaging 3.5 arrests and 9.5 weeks of confinement prior to program entry. In evaluating FANS, Henggeler, Melton, and Smith (1992) compared program youth with control group youth who were on normal probation and had similar offense histories. More than a year after the project began, significant differences were found between the FANS and control groups in the following areas, among others: absence of rearrest (FANS: 58 percent; control: 38 percent) and subsequent confinement (FANS: 20 percent; control: 68 percent). In addition, FANS youth experienced increased family cohesion and reduced aggression with peers, and the FANS program was judged cost effective, at about a fifth the cost of institutional placement.

MST is a model program of the OJJDP-funded Blueprints for Violence Prevention project (see Mihalic et al., 2001). For additional information, contact:

Marshall E. Swenson
Manager of Program Development
MST Services
710 J. Dodds Boulevard
Mt. Pleasant, SC 29464
843–856–8226
843–856–8227
marshall.swenson@mstservices.com
www.mstservices.com

Scott Henggeler, Ph.D.
Family Services Research Center
Department of Psychiatry and Behavioral Sciences
Medical University of South Carolina
171 Ashley Avenue
Charleston, SC 29425
843–876–1800
843–876–1808 (fax)
heggesw@musc.edu

Residential treatment. Community residential centers provide 24-hour supervision of offenders, usually nonviolent offenders. Studies in the 1970s of group homes found that they either performed better or no worse than state institutions in reducing recidivism. However, Lipsey and Wilson's (1998) review of the literature found that teaching family homes (where a small number of delinquents live with supervising adults who focus on modifying behaviors) were effective in reducing recidivism. This type of program was one of only two interventions out of 83 studied shown to be consistently effective in reducing recidivism among institutionalized youth. Teaching family homes produced an approximately 30–35 percent reduction in recidivism rates (juveniles not receiving treatment had a recidivism rate of 50 percent).

Treatment foster care (TFC) programs use adult mentors and nondelinquent peers to isolate delinquent youth from the negative influences of criminally involved peers. Youth receive treatment and intensive supervision at home, in school, and in the community. TFC also provides services to the youth's biological family with the ultimate goal of family reunification. TFC programs target youth with serious and chronic histories of delinquent behavior who are at risk of confinement. Evaluations have demonstrated that, compared with control group youth, TFC youth spent 60 percent fewer days in confinement over a 12-month period, ran away from the program three times less often (on average), and used drugs less often (Chamberlain and Mihalic, 1998).

Another model program is VisionQuest. Founded in 1973, VisionQuest is a national program through which serious juvenile offenders spend several months in outdoor programs, such as wilderness camps, followed by 5 months in a residential home in the community. The group home component prepares youth for reintegration into their families and communities by formulating education goals, improving relationships with family members, and establishing plans for the future. As a multidimensional program, it is not possible to separate the effects of the outdoor program from the group home experience. Greenwood and Turner (1987) evaluated San Diego, CA's VisionQuest by comparing program youth with offenders who had been incarcerated in a county correctional institution.[9] Although the VisionQuest group contained more serious offenders than the control group, offenders in the former were less likely to be rearrested during the year after release (55 percent versus 71 percent). After controlling for differences in group characteristics, the VisionQuest group were about half as likely to reoffend as the previously incarcerated group.

For additional information, contact:

VisionQuest National, Ltd.
600 North Swan Road
P.O. Box 12906
Tucson, AZ 85732
520–881–3950
visionquest@vq.com
www.vq.com

Common Characteristics of Promising and Effective Program Initiatives

The existing body of research suggests that, overall, community-based alternatives to secure detention and long-term confinement of juvenile offenders tend to be at least as successful in reducing recidivism as traditional detention and confinement. The literature evaluating various alternatives is uneven and mixed, but some general conclusions can be drawn regarding programs that appear to produce positive results.

The most successful programs are based on interventions that are intensive (involving frequent contacts with offenders), sustained (involving continuous monitoring for a substantial period of time), holistic (covering several aspects of the juvenile's life), and linked to serious rehabilitative services (Dryfoos, 1990; MacKenzie, 1997). Krisberg and Howell's (1998:360) survey of research concluded that "alternatives to secure confinement for serious and chronic juveniles are at least as effective in suppressing recidivism as incarceration, but are considerably less costly to operate." They identified nine studies of community-based alternatives to confinement that appear to demonstrate that such alternatives perform well in reducing recidivism. However, only three of these studies used randomized experimental designs.

---

[9] Although more recent data were unavailable at the time this Bulletin was written, a description of VisionQuest was included here because the program remains one of the most well-known and best regarded.

By contrast, programs that are unsuccessful in reducing recidivism include deterrence programs such as boot camps and "shock" probation programs (e.g., Scared Straight), and individual or group counseling sessions that lack clear plans to address offenders' problems (Andrews et al., 1990; Dryfoos, 1990; Jensen and Rojek, 1992; Lipsey, 1992; Lipsey and Wilson, 1998; MacKenzie, 1997). MacKenzie (1997) found a preponderance of evidence showing that the boot camp and shock types of deterrence programs either did not affect subsequent offending or actually increased recidivism. Similarly, most wilderness programs for juveniles have not been shown to effectively reduce recidivism.

Results are mixed for intensive supervision, home confinement, and community residential programs: their success depends on the inclusion of appropriate rehabilitative services. Structured rehabilitative treatments focused on specific skills and behaviors appear to have beneficial effects regardless of where they take place.

Lipsey's (1992) meta-analysis of 443 studies of juvenile programs (both inside correctional institutions and in community-based environments) found that treatment programs that were employment- or behavior-oriented and that provided multimodal treatment were the most successful. His analysis also indicated that rehabilitative treatments in community settings reduced recidivism more effectively than treatments in custodial institutions, though Lipsey notes that further research is needed to sort out possible confounding factors. Lipsey classified studies into several "treatment modality" categories and statistically evaluated their effectiveness in reducing recidivism. Following are the categories in order of effectiveness, with the estimated percentage of recidivism rates for treatment and control groups, respectively:

♦ Employment (32/50).

♦ Multimodal (38/50).

♦ Behavioral (38/50).

♦ Skill oriented (40/50).

♦ Community residential (42/50).

♦ Release, probation/parole (45/50).

♦ Reduced caseload, probation/parole (46/50).

♦ Restitution, probation/parole (46/50).

♦ Individual counseling (46/50).

♦ Group counseling (47/50).

♦ Other enhancement, probation/parole (47/50).

♦ Family counseling (49/50).

♦ Vocational training (59/50).

♦ Deterrence programs (62/50).

Lipsey and Wilson (1998) conducted an updated 1998 meta-analysis of 117 programs targeting serious offenders but found no significant differences in the effectiveness of treatment programs based in the community and those operating within institutions. However, this does not undermine Lipsey's earlier finding regarding the possible benefits of community-based alternatives because he includes within the "institutional" category residential treatment centers, group homes, and camps in addition to more traditional correctional facilities (Lipsey and Wilson, 1998).

Among the interventions for noninstitutionalized serious offenders, interpersonal skills training, individual counseling, and behavioral programs have consistently shown strong positive effects in reducing recidivism (Lipsey and Wilson, 1998). Multiple service programs and restitution ordered as the sole condition of parole/probation were less effective. Wilderness/challenge programs, early release from probation/parole, deterrence, and vocational programs were clearly ineffective. The effectiveness of academic programs, advocacy casework, and family counseling was unclear. Based on the 1998 analysis, recidivism figures for the most successful programs, compared with recidivism rates among the control group, were as follows:

- Individual counseling (28/50).

- Interpersonal skills (29/50).

- Behavioral programs (30/50).

- Multiple services (36/50).

- Employment (39/50).

Some important caveats should be borne in mind when evaluating findings in the literature on alternatives to incarceration, particularly with regard to reported recidivism rates for traditional correctional versus alternative programs. Many of the alternative programs, such as intensive supervision and day reporting, may result in greater scrutiny of offenders and, hence, higher rates of reported recidivism. This might account for the lack of significant differences found in some studies between these programs and more traditional approaches. Higher or similar recidivism rates for youth in alternative programs compared with youth in traditional detention and confinement may be, at least in part, a "program effect" rather than a substantive program weakness. For example, because ISPs impose greater supervision and often more constraints than traditional forms of probation, participating offenders have a greater number of technical violations and thus returns to correctional institutions. When combined with treatment programs and other services, however, evidence exists that recidivism is reduced (Parent et al., 1995).

Another important issue is the extent to which program participants have been selected appropriately according to an objective assessment of risk and needs. As noted throughout this document, the way in which offenders are assessed and targeted has everything to do with the extent to which programs will produce quality outcomes and whether their cost effectiveness can be demonstrated. Unfortunately, not all alternative programs utilize quality risk assessment and classification systems, leaving them vulnerable to competing theories about the reasoning behind the outcomes produced. For example, if an ISP is determined to be effective in reducing recidivism but does not document the proper selection of program participants, it could be argued that the program simply accepted offenders who were not at high risk of reoffending to begin with. Thus, program integrity, and the quality and usefulness of outcome evaluations, depends on the certainty with which the program was delivered to its intended target population. The success of alternative programs rests on the careful selection of appropriate clients (via risk and needs assessment) and the delivery of sound programming that responds to the constellation of needs for services and supervision that individual youth present.

Conclusion

Despite recent decreases in juvenile crime, many jurisdictions continue to struggle with crowding in their detention and secure confinement facilities. In addition to the negative impact of crowding on the facility's ability to deliver quality programming and to maintain safety and security, it is quite clear that many youth do not require secure detention or confinement to ensure their appearance in court or to prevent future reoffending. To reduce their reliance on these types of programs, jurisdictions must develop and use objective assessment tools and make available a continuum of evidence-based programs.

Current literature offers insight into the types of programs shown to be most effective in deterring juvenile crime and in addressing the root causes of delinquency. Most of these do not feature secure custodial settings but instead work with youth in the communities in which they live, go to school, and work. Further, the use of objective classification and risk assessment instruments at various decision points in the juvenile justice system has been shown to lead to the appropriate alternative placement of juvenile offenders without compromising public safety. These reforms can be achieved by several methods. Whether through new program initiatives or legislation-, administrative-, or litigation-based reforms, each jurisdiction bears the responsibility for enhancing its programmatic alternatives to meet the needs of the youth it serves.

References

Andrews, D., Zinger, I., Hoge, R., Bonta, J., Gendreau, P., and Cullen, F. 1990. Does correctional treatment work? A clinically relevant and psychologically informed meta-analysis. *Criminology* 28(3):369–404.

Annie E. Casey Foundation. 2000. *Pathways to Juvenile Detention Reform*. Baltimore, MD: Annie E. Casey Foundation.

Arthur, L. 2001. Ten ways to reduce detention populations. *Juvenile and Family Court Journal* 52(1):29–36.

Austin, J. 2001. *Controlling Prison Population Growth Through Alternatives to Incarceration: Lessons Learned From BJA's Corrections Options Demonstration Program*. Report. Washington, DC: U.S. Department of Justice, Office of Justice Programs, Bureau of Justice Assistance.

Austin, J., and Krisberg, B. 1982. Unmet promise of alternatives to incarceration. *Crime and Delinquency* 28(3):374–409.

Baird, S.C., Sturrs, G., Connelly, H. 1984. *Classification of Juveniles in Corrections—A Model Systems Approach*. Report. Washington, DC: U.S. Department of Justice, Office of Justice Programs, Office of Juvenile Justice and Delinquency Prevention.

Ball, R., Huff, C., and Lilly, J. 1988. *House Arrest and Correctional Policy: Doing Time at Home*. Beverly Hills, CA: Sage Publications.

Barton, W., and Butts, J. 1990. Accommodating innovation in a juvenile court. *Criminal Justice Policy Review* 4(2):144–158.

Chamberlain, P., and Mihalic, S. 1998. *Blueprints for Violence Prevention. Book Eight: Multidimensional Treatment Foster Care*. Boulder, CO: Center for the Study and Prevention of Violence.

Coates, R., Miller, A., and Ohlin, L. 1978. *Diversity in a Youth Correctional System*. Cambridge, MA: Ballinger.

Cohn, A., Biondi, L., Flaim, L.C., Paskowski, M., and Cohn, S. 1997. Evaluating electronic monitoring programs. *Alternatives to Incarceration* 3(1):16–24.

Cullen, F., and Gendreau, P. 2000. Assessing correctional rehabilitation: Policy, practice, and prospects. In *Criminal Justice 2000*, vol. 3, edited by J. Horney. Washington, DC: U.S. Department of Justice, Office of Justice Programs, National Institute of Justice, pp. 109–160.

Davidson, W., Amdur, R.L., Mitchell, C.M., and Redner, R. 1990. *Alternative Treatments for Troubled Youth: The Case of Diversion From the Justice System*. New York, NY: Plenum Press.

Dryfoos, J. 1990. *Adolescents at Risk: Prevalence and Prevention*. New York, NY: Oxford University Press.

Ezell, M. 1992. Juvenile diversion: The ongoing search for alternatives. In *Juvenile Justice and Public Policy*, edited by I. Schwartz. New York, NY: Lexington.

Fagan, J. 1996. The comparative advantage of juvenile versus criminal court sanctions on recidivism among adolescent felony offenders. *Law and Policy* 18(1 and 2):77–113.

Fratto, J., and Hallstrom, D. 1978. Conditional release and intensive supervision programs. *Juvenile and Family Court Journal* 29(4):29–35.

Greenwood, P., and Turner, S. 1993. Evaluation of the Paint Creek Youth Center: A residential program for serious delinquents. *Criminology* 31(2):263–279.

Greenwood, P., and Turner, S. 1987. *The VisionQuest Program: An Evaluation*. Santa Monica, CA: RAND.

Hardyman, P. 1999. *Georgia Department of Juvenile Justice External Classification System Users Manual*. Washington, DC: The Institute on Crime, Justice and Corrections at The George Washington University.

Harms, P. 2003. *Detention in Delinquency Cases, 1990–1999*. Fact Sheet. Washington, DC: U.S. Department of Justice, Office of Justice Programs, Office of Juvenile Justice and Delinquency Prevention.

Henggeler, S. 1997. *Treating Serious Anti-Social Behavior in Youth: The MST Approach*. Bulletin. Washington, DC: U.S. Department of Justice, Office of Justice Programs, Office of Juvenile Justice and Delinquency Prevention.

Henggeler, S., Melton, G., and Smith, L. 1992. Family preservation using multisystemic therapy: An effective alternative to incarcerating serious juvenile offenders. *Journal of Consulting and Clinical Psychology* 60(6):953–961.

Henggeler, S., Mihalic, S.F., Rone, L., Thomas, C., and Timmons-Mitchell, J. 1998. Multisystemic therapy. In *Blueprints for Violence Prevention*, edited by D. Elliot. Boulder, CO: Center for the Study and Prevention of Violence, Institute of Behavioral Sciences, University of Colorado at Boulder.

Howell, J.C. 1995. *Guide for Implementing the Comprehensive Strategy for Serious, Violent and Chronic Juvenile Offenders*. Report. Washington, DC: U.S. Department of Justice, Office of Justice Programs, Office of Juvenile Justice and Delinquency Prevention.

Jensen, G., and Rojek, D. 1992. *Delinquency and Youth Crime*. Prospect Heights, IL: Waveland Press.

Johnson, K., Wagner, D., and Matthews, T. 2002. *Missouri Juvenile Risk Assessment Re-Validation Report*. Madison, WI: National Council on Crime and Delinquency.

Kazdin, A., and Weisz, J. 1998. Identifying and developing empirically supported child and adolescent treatments. *Journal of Consulting and Clinical Psychology* 66(1):19–36.

Kihm, R., and Block, J. 1982. Response to a crisis: Reducing the juvenile detention rate in Louisville, Kentucky. *Juvenile and Family Court Journal* 33(1):37–44.

Krisberg, B. 1997. *The Impact of the Juvenile Justice System on Serious, Violent and Chronic Juvenile Offenders*. San Francisco, CA: National Council on Crime and Delinquency.

Krisberg, B., Austin, J., and Steele, P. 1989. *Unlocking Juvenile Corrections*. San Francisco, CA: National Council on Crime and Delinquency.

Krisberg, B., and Howell, J. 1998. The impact of the juvenile justice system and prospects for graduated sanctions in a comprehensive strategy. In *Serious and Violent Juvenile Offenders*, edited by R. Loeber and D. Farrington. Thousand Oaks, CA: Sage.

Land, K., McCall, P., and Parker, K. 1994. Logistic versus hazards regression analyses in evaluation research: An exposition and application to the North Carolina Court Counselors' Intensive Protective Supervision Project. *Evaluation Review* 18(4):411–437.

Land, K., McCall, P., and Williams, J. 1990. Something that works in juvenile justice: An evaluation of the North Carolina Court Counselors' Intensive Supervision Project, 1987–1989. *Evaluation Review* 14(6):574–606.

Lipsey, M. 1992. Juvenile delinquency treatment: A meta-analytic inquiry into the variability of effects. In *Community Crime Prevention: Does it Work?* edited by D. Rosenbaum. New York, NY: Russell Sage Foundation.

Lipsey, M., and Wilson, D. 1998. Effective intervention for serious juvenile offenders. In *Serious and Violent Juvenile Offenders*, edited by R. Loeber and D. Farrington. Thousand Oaks, CA: Sage.

Lubow, B. 1999. Successful strategies for reforming juvenile detention. *Federal Probation* 63(2):16–24.

MacKenzie, D. 1997. Criminal justice and crime prevention. In *Preventing Crime: What Works, What Doesn't, What's Promising*. Washington, DC: U.S. Department of Justice, Office of Justice Programs, National Institute of Justice.

Mears, D. 2001. Critical challenges in addressing the mental health needs of juvenile offenders. *Justice Policy Journal* 1(1):41–61.

Mihalic, S., Irwin, K., Elliott, D., Fagan, A., and Hansen, D. 2001. *Blueprints for Violence Prevention*. Bulletin. Washington, DC: U.S. Department of Justice, Office of Justice Programs, Office of Juvenile Justice and Delinquency Prevention.

Murray, C., and Cox, L. 1979. *Beyond Probation*. Beverly Hills, CA: Sage.

Parent, D., Byrne, J., Tsarfaty, V., Valade, L., and Esselman, J. 1995. *Day Reporting Centers*. Monograph. Washington, DC: U.S. Department of Justice, Office of Justice Programs, National Institute of Justice.

Puzzanchera, C. 2003. *Juvenile Court Placement of Adjudicated Youth, 1990–1999.* Bulletin. Washington, DC: U.S. Department of Justice, Office of Justice Programs, Office of Juvenile Justice and Delinquency Prevention.

Rojek, D. 1986. Juvenile diversion and the potential of inappropriate treatment for offenders. *New England Journal on Criminal and Civil Confinement* 12(2):329–347.

Roy, S. 1997. Five years of electronic monitoring of adults and juveniles in Lake County, Indiana. *Journal of Crime and Justice* 20(1):141–160.

Roy, S., and Brown, M. 1995. Juvenile electronic monitoring program in Lake County, Indiana: An evaluation. In *Intermediate Sanctions: Sentencing in the 1990s*, edited by J. Smykla and W. Selke. Cincinnati, OH: Anderson Publishing.

Shelden, R. 1999. *Detention Diversion Advocacy: An Evaluation*. Bulletin. Washington, DC: U.S. Department of Justice, Office of Justice Programs, Office of Juvenile Justice and Delinquency Prevention.

Sickmund, M. 2002. *Juvenile Residential Facility Census, 2000: Selected Findings*. Bulletin. Washington, DC: U.S. Department of Justice, Office of Justice Programs, Office of Juvenile Justice and Delinquency Prevention.

Smykla, J., and Selke, W. 1982. Impact of home detention: A less restrictive alternative to the detention of juveniles. *Juvenile and Family Court Journal* 33(2):3–9.

Snyder, H., and Sickmund, M. 1999. *Juvenile Offenders and Victims: 1999 National Report.* Report. Washington, DC: U.S. Department of Justice, Office of Justice Programs, Office of Juvenile Justice and Delinquency Prevention.

Sontheimer, H., and Goodstein, L. 1993. Evaluation of juvenile intensive aftercare probation. *Justice Quarterly* 10(2):197–227.

Stanfield, R. 2000. *Pathways to Juvenile Detention Reform Overview*. Baltimore, MD: Annie E. Casey Foundation.

Stanford, R. 1984. Implementing the multigoal evaluation technique in diversion programs. In *Juvenile Justice Policy: Analyzing Trends and Outcomes*, edited by S. Decker. Beverly Hills, CA: Sage.

Thornton, T.N., Craft, C.A., Dahlberg, L.L., Lynch, B.S., and Baer, K. 2000. *Best Practices of Youth Violence Prevention: A Sourcebook for Community Action*. Atlanta, GA: Centers for Disease Control and Prevention, National Center for Injury Prevention and Control.

Torbet, P. 1999. *Holding Juvenile Offenders Accountable: Programming Needs of Juvenile Probation Departments*. Pittsburgh, PA: National Center for Juvenile Justice.

Vaughn, J. 1989. A survey of juvenile electronic monitoring and home confinement programs. *Juvenile and Family Court Journal* 40(4):1–36

Wasserman, G., Ko, S., McReynolds, L. 2004. *Assessing the Mental Health Status of Youth in Juvenile Justice Settings*. Bulletin. Washington, DC: U.S. Department of Justice, Office of Justice Programs, Office of Juvenile Justice and Delinquency Prevention.

Wiebush, R. 1993. Juvenile intensive supervision: The impact on felony offenders diverted from institutional placement. *Crime and Delinquency* 39(1):68–89.

Wiebush, R., Baird, C., Krisberg, B., and Onek, D. 1995. Risk assessment and classification for serious, violent, and chronic juvenile offenders. In *A Sourcebook: Serious, Violent, and Chronic Juvenile Offenders*, edited by J. Howell, B. Krisberg, D. Hawkins, and J. Wilson. Thousand Oaks, CA: Sage Publications.

Wiebush, R., Wagner, D., McNulty, B., Wang, Y., and Le, T. 2005. *Implementation and Outcome Evaluation of the Intensive Aftercare Program*. Report. Washington, DC: U.S. Department of Justice, Office of Justice Programs, Office of Juvenile Justice and Delinquency Prevention.

Winner, L., Lanza-Kaduce, L., Bishop, D., and Frazier, C. 1997. The transfer of juveniles to criminal courts: Reexamining recidivism rates over the long term. *Crime and Delinquency* 43(4):548–563.

Young, T.M., and Pappenfort, D.M. 1979. *Use of Secure Detention for Juveniles and Alternatives to Its Use*. Report. Washington, DC: U.S. Department of Justice, Office of Justice Programs, National Institute of Justice.

Acknowledgments

James Austin, Ph.D., is the President of JFA Associates, LLC, in Washington, DC. Kelly Dedel Johnson, Ph.D., is Director of One in 37 Research, Inc., in Portland, OR. Ronald Weitzer, Ph.D., is a professor of sociology at The George Washington University in Washington, DC.

This Bulletin was prepared under contract number OJP-2000-298-BF from the Office of Juvenile Justice and Delinquency Prevention.

The Office of Juvenile Justice and Delinquency Prevention is a component of the Office of Justice Programs, which also includes the Bureau of Justice Assistance, the Bureau of Justice Statistics, the National Institute of Justice, and the Office for Victims of Crime.

NCJ 208804

Appendixes

A.   Cook County Juvenile Probation Department Risk Assessment Instrument
Adapted from Annie E. Casey Foundation, 2000

B.   Georgia Department of Juvenile Justice Detention Assessment Instrument
Source: Georgia Department of Juvenile Justice

C.   Louisiana Office of Juvenile Services Secure Custody Screening Document
Source: Wiebush et al., 1995

D.   Indiana Juvenile Corrections Placement Matrix (Proposed)
Source: Wiebush et al., 1995

E.   Georgia Department of Juvenile Justice Custody Assessment System: Initial Assessment
Source: Georgia Department of Juvenile Justice

F.   Georgia Department of Juvenile Justice Custody Assessment System: Reassessment
Source: Georgia Department of Juvenile Justice

G.   Georgia Department of Juvenile Justice Housing Assignment Matrix
Source: Georgia Department of Juvenile Justice

H.   Juvenile Probation and Aftercare Sample Risk Assessment Instrument
Source: Wiebush et al., 1995

Appendix A: Cook County Juvenile Probation Department Risk Assessment Instrument

Screen Date: ____/____/____   Screen Time:_____a.m./p.m.   Screener: _____

Youth Officer: _____   District: _____

Minor Respondent: _____   DOB: _____   Age: _____

Sex: M / F   Race: White / Black / Hispanic / Asian / Other   YD: _____

Factor (Choose only one item per factor.)	Score
1. Most Serious Instant Offense_____	
Automatic transfer cases	15
Violent felonies (murder, armed robbery with handgun, home invasion, ACSA, UUW-gun, agg. batt.—bodily harm, agg. vehicular invasion, agg. discharge of a firearm, agg. battery with a firearm)	15
Other forc ble felonies (robbery, kidnapping, intimidation, CSA, hate crime, agg. batt., vehicular invasion)	10
Other offenses	
Felony sale of cannabis (class 1 or 2 felony amount), arson, DCS	10
PCS w/intent to deliver, residential burglary, UUW (no gun), possession of explosives	7
Felony possession of narcotics/drugs for sale or other felonies	5
Misdemeanor possession of narcotics/drugs or other weapons possession	3
Other misdemeanors	2
Not picked up on new offense (warrant)	0
2. Prior Court Referrals	
Prior IDOC commitment	7
Prior court referral within the last 24-hour period	5
Prior court referral within the last 7 days	4
Six or more total court referrals within the last 12 months (#___)	2
No court referrals within the last 12 months	0
3. Past Findings of Delinquency-Closed Proceedings	
Past finding of delinquency on a violent felony	5
Past finding of delinquency on a felony	4
Past finding of delinquency on a misdemeanor (# of findings x 1 up to a total of 3 points)	1 / 2 / 3
No past finding of delinquency	0
4. Current Case Status	
IPS	6
Probation (#___) Supervision (#___) Multiple Dispo Dates	5
Probation (#___) Supervision (#___) Single Dispo Date	3
Not an active case	0
5. Petitions Pending Adjudication	
3+ petitions pending (#___)	3
2 petitions pending	2
1 petition pending	1
No petitions pending	0
6. Under Preadjudicatory Order of Home Confinement	4
7. Warrant Cases	
Category 1: Mandatory detention	15
Category 2: Nonmandatory detention	8
8. Violation of Juvenile Electronic Monitoring	15
Total Score	_____

Decision Scale

Score 0–9   Authorize Release (with notice of prioritized date for 5–12 conference)

Score 10–14   Complete Nonsecure Detention Options Form

Score 15+   Authorize Detention (for minors age 13 and older)
              (Complete nonsecure custody options for minors younger than age 13 before placement in secure detention)

Administrative Override (supervisory approval is required)

No/Yes (reason) _____

Final Decision

Detain   Release   Release With Conditions

Appendix B: Georgia Department of Juvenile Justice
Detention Assessment Instrument

===

Youth's Name: _____ DOB: ____/____/____ DJJ #: _____

Gender: 1. Male 2. Female   Race: 1. White 2. African-American 3. Hispanic 4. Asian 5. Other:_____

Worker: _____ County:_____ Date: ____/____/____ Time: _____ a.m./p.m.

===

The purpose of the Detention Assessment Instrument is to provide greater consistency and equity in detention decisionmaking. The criteria used reflect an emphasis on public safety concerns. The instrument helps operationalize the detention criteria specified in OCGA 15-11-18 and 15-11-18.1. Complete the assessment for all initial detention decisions.

A. Reason for Detention Referral (check all that apply)

1.__ New Offense Alleged 2. __ Court Detention Order/Warrant 3. __ DJJ Apprehension Order 4. __ Other:_____

	Point Value	Score

B. Detention Assessment

1. Detention/Apprehension Order Status

	Point Value	Score
Current detention referral includes court detention order/warrant or DJJ apprehension order	15	
Current detention referral based on new charge only	0	
		_____

2. Most Serious Current Charge _____ _____
              (Offense name)   (DJJ Offense Code)

Class I: Aggravated sexual battery; agg. child molestation; agg. sodomy; armed robbery with firearm; murder; rape; voluntary manslaughter   15

Class II: Agg. assault; kidnapping; att. kidnapping; att. murder; arson (1st and 2d degree); agg. battery; robbery; carry weapon to school; child molestation; highjacking; poss/sale of schedule I or II drugs   15

Class III: Escape by force or w/weapon; vehicular homicide; poss/sale of schedule III, IV, or V drugs; poss/use schedule I, II drugs; poss >100 bs marijuana; 1st degree criminal damage; cruelty to children   12

           10

Class IV: Escape; arson (3rd deg); burglary; invol. manslaughter; poss/sale/use >1oz but <100 lbs marijuana; assault teacher   8

Class V: All other felony offenses   6

Class VI: All misdemeanor offenses   4

Class VII: Status or administrative offenses (technical violation of probation, DJJ placement, parole/aftercare)   2

No new charge; court detention order/warrant or DJJ apprehension order ONLY   0

           _____

3. Additional Current Charges

	Point Value	Score
Two or more additional current felony charges (actual #: _____)	3	
One additional felony charge	2	
One or more additional misdemeanor, or status offense, or VOP charges	1	
No additional current charges	0	
		_____

4. Additional Charges Pending Adjudication

	Point Value	Score
3+ additional pending charges (actual #: _____)	3	
2 additional pending charges	2	
1 additional pending charge	1	
No other pending charges	0	
		_____

5. Prior Adjudicated Charges

	Point Value	Score
2+ prior adjudications for violent felony offenses (Class I - IV)	6	
3+ prior adjudications for felony charges (actual #: _____)	5	
2 prior adjudications for felony charges	4	
1 prior adjudication for a felony charge	3	
2+ prior adjudications for misdemeanor charges (actual #: _____)	2	
1 prior adjudication for misdemeanor	1	
No prior felony or misdemeanor adjudications, but one or more adjudications for status offenses	1	
No prior adjudications	0	
		_____

6. Prior Escapes, Runaways, or Failures to Appear

	Point Value	Score
Youth has had one or more court orders/warrants or DJJ apprehension orders for escape, runaway, or failure to appear (FTA)	3	
No prior court orders/warrants or DJJ apprehension orders for escape, runaway, or FTA	0	
		_____

7. Current Legal Status

	Point Value	Score
Committed to DJJ as a designated felon	5	
Committed to DJJ for a delinquent offense	3	
On probation for delinquency or committed as a status offender	2	
On probation for status offense	1	
No current legal status	0	
		_____

8. Total Detention Assessment Score   _____

C. Detention Decision

9. Assessment-Indicated Initial Detention Decision

Score	Level	Indicated Decision
12 or higher	_____ 3	Detain
8–11	_____ 2	Release to alternative program
2–7	_____ 1	Release to parent, guardian, or other respons ble adult

10. Override to Indicated Decision (check override type and note applicable reasons)

_____ No override

_____ Detain pending court approval for alternative placement

_____ Mandatory court policy override (only as specified per DJJ-local court agreement)
Indicate applicable policy: _____

_____ DJJ policy override (check all applicable items)

Aggravating Factors (override to detention)

____ Explicit threat to flee if released

____ Poss./use firearm during offense

____ Actual/threatened mass school violence

____ Interstate case

____ Other: _____

Aggravating Factors (override to detention alternative)

____ Parents unwilling/unable to provide close supervision

____ Child may be in danger if returned home

____ Intercounty case

____ Other: _____

Mitigating Factors (override to less restrictive placement)

____ Multiple ("stacked") charges from one incident

____ Youth marginally involved in offense

____ No offenses in past 6 months

____ Parent willing/able to provide close supervision

____ Offense less serious than indicated by charge

____ Other: _____

Override justification/explanation:

_____

_____

_____

11. Initial Detention Decision	12. Court Detention Decision (48/72 Hr Hearing)

___ Detain Specify RYDC: _____
 	
 ___ Release to alternative
      ___ Contract Home
      ___ Intensive Super
      ___ House-bound
      ___ Other: _____
 	
 ___ Unconditional release
 	
 If released to alternative or unconditional, indicate to whom released:
 	
 Name: _____
 	
 Relationship: _____
 	
 Address: _____
 	
          _____
 	
 Phone: _____
	Hearing Date: _____/_____/_____ _____ Not Applicable
	            (released initially)
	 ____ Continue detention
	
	 ____ Release to alternative
	      ____ Contract Home
	      ____ Intensive Super
	      ____ House-bound
	      ____ Other: _____
	
	 ____ Unconditional release
	
	 If released to alternative or unconditional, indicate to whom released:
	
	 Name: _____
	
	 Relationship: _____
	
	 Address: _____
	
	          _____
	
	 Phone: _____

Appendix C: Louisiana Office of Juvenile Services Secure Custody Screening Document

                                                                                          Score

1. Severity of Present Adjudicated Offense

   Level 0 felony = 10   Level 3 felony = 3
   Level 1 felony = 7   Level 4 felony = 1
   Level 2 felony = 5   All other = 0

                                                                                          _____

2. If Present Adjudication Involves

   Possession/Use of firearm = 2
   Multiple felonies = 2

                                                                                          _____

3. Number of Prior Adjudications

   Two or more felony adjudications = 2
   One felony or two or more misdemeanors = 1
   None = 0

                                                                                          _____

4. Most Serious Prior Adjudication

   Level 0 or Level 1 felony = 5
   Level 2 felony = 3
   Level 3 felony = 0

                                                                                          _____

5. For Offenders With Prior Adjudications

   Age at first adjudication:
       Age 13 or younger = 2
       Age 14 = 1
       Age 15 or older = 0

                                                                                          _____

6. History of Probation/Parole Supervision

   Offender currently on probation/parole = 2
   Offender with probation/parole revocation = 1

                                                                                          _____

7. History of In-Home/Nonsecure Residential Intervention

   Three or more prior failures = 3
   One or two prior failures = 1
   None = 0

                                                                                          _____

8. If the Offender Had a Prior Placement in OJS = 2

                                                                                          _____

9. Prior Escapes or Runaways

   From secure more than once = 3
   From secure once or nonsecure two or more times = 2
   From nonsecure once = 0

                                                                                          _____

                                                               Total Score   _____

Recommended Actions

0–6 = Consider nonsecure placement
7–8 = Consider short-term secure placement
9 or more = Consider secure placement

Appendix D: Indiana Juvenile Corrections
Placement Matrix (Proposed)

Offense Severity	Risk Level		
	High	Medium	Low
Violent offenses	Violent offender program; assaultive sex offender program; staff-secure residential	Violent or sex offender program; staff-secure residential	Boot camp; intermediate sanctions program
Serious offenses	Boot camp; staff-secure residential; job corps; intermediate sanctions program	Intermediate sanctions program	Intermediate sanctions program; day treatment; specialized group homes
Less serious offenses	Intermediate sanctions program; day treatment; specialized group homes	Proctor program; tracking; community service	Community supervision; community service; mentor
Minor offenses	Proctor program; tracking; community supervision	Community supervision; mentor	Mentor

Appendix E: Georgia Department of Juvenile Justice
Custody Assessment System: Initial Assessment

I. Identification

Name: _____ DJJ ID#: _____ SSN#: _____

Facility: _____ DOB: _____ Gender: Male / Female

Race: Black/NH White/NH Other/NH White-Hispanic Black-Hispanic Other-Hispanic Am. Indian/Alaskan
     Asian/Pacific Islander

II. Initial Assessment

1. Severity of Current Charge/Adjudication
   - Superior court/Person-to-person offense with injury 4
   - Weapons offense/Person-to-person offense without injury 3
   - Felony property/Drug-related offense 2
   - Misdemeanor offense 1

   _____

2. Type of Prior Institutional Commitments or Placements (include short term, RYDCs, YDCs, and out-of home placements)
   - Commitment to state youth development campus 4
   - Prior short-term program 3
   - Prior residential placement by court, DFACS, or DJJ 2
   - Prior residential placement by parent/guardian or no prior out-of-home placements 0

   _____

3. Number of Runaways/Escapes From Prior Placements
   - One or more 2
   - None 0

   _____

4. Current Age
   - 18 + ... 3
   - 15 to 17 2
   - 12 to 14 1
   - 11 or younger 0

   _____

5. Severity of Prior Adjudications
   - Superior court/ Person-to person offense with injury 3
   - Weapons charge/Person-to-person offense without injury 2
   - Felony property/Drug-related/Misdemeanor offense 1
   - Status/Traffic offense 0

   _____

6. Severity of Prior Institutional Misconduct Reports
   - Predatory major with injury, closed unit placements, and/or new charges filed 4
   - Nonpredatory major 2
   - Minor 1
   - None 0

   _____

7. Number of Prior Authorized Institutional Misconduct Reports (during last 2 calendar years)
   - 13 or more 3
   - 7 to 12 2
   - 2 to 6 1
   - 0 to 1 0

Total Score _____

III. **Custody Assessment** (Circle the appropriate level.)

Minimum   0–8 on Items 1–7
Medium   9–13 on Items 1–7
High   14 on Items 1–7

IV. **Mandatory Overrides** (Circle all that are applicable. Explain below in comments.)

Current superior court case   Institutional predatory offense (rape, sexual/agg. assault)
Pending superior court case   High-profile/Notorious case
Institutional referral to DA

V. **Discretionary Override** (Circle all that are applicable. Explain below in comments.)

Poor institutional performance   Protective custody
Mental health risk   Exceptional institutional performance
Suicide risk   Medical needs _____
Mental disability

VI. **Recommended Custody Level** (Circle appropriate level.)

Minimum   Medium   High   Special Management

Signature: _____ Date:_____/_____/_____ Time: _____a.m./p.m.

VII. **Supervisor-Approved Custody Level** (Approval required if override indicated. Circle appropriate level.)

Minimum   Medium   High   Special Management

Supervisor Signature: _____ Date:_____/_____/_____ Time: _____a.m./p.m.

VIII. **Comments**

Appendix F: Georgia Department of Juvenile Justice
Custody Assessment System: Reassessment

I. Identification

Name: _____ DJJ ID#:_____ SSN#:_____

Facility: _____ DOB:_____ Gender: Male / Female

Race: Black/NH White/NH Other/NH White-Hispanic Black-Hispanic Other-Hispanic Am. Indian/Alaskan
    Asian/Pacific Islander

Date of Prior Assessment: _____   Current level: MIN   MED   HIGH   SM   Room: _____

II. Reassessment

1. Severity of Current Charge/Adjudication
    Superior court/Person-to-person offense with injury 3
    Weapons charge/Person-to-person offense without injury 2
    Property/Drug-related offense 1
    Misdemeanor, status, or traffic offense 0
    _____

2. Type of Prior Institutional Commitments or Placements (include short term, RYDCs, YDCs, and out-of home placements)
    Commitment to state youth development campus 2
    Prior short-term program 1
    Prior residential placement by court, DFACS, or DJJ 0
    No prior court-ordered out-of-home placements 0
    _____

3. Current Age
    18 + ... 2
    15 to 17 1
    12 to 14 0
    11 or younger .... −1
    _____

4. Severity of Prior Adjudications
    Superior court/Person-to-person offense with injury 2
    Person-to-person offense without injury/Weapons/Drug-related offense 1
    Felony property, any misdemeanor, status, traffic offense 0
    _____

5. Severity of Institutional Misconduct Reports
    1+ predatory major report, closed unit placement and/or new charges filed during past 90 days 6
    1+ predatory major report, closed unit placement and/or new charges filed during past year 4
    1+ nonpredatory major report during past 6 months 2
    1+ minor report during past 90 days 1
    None 0
    _____

6. Number of Institutional Misconduct Reports During Past 90 Days
    13 or more 3
    7 to 12 2
    2 to 6 1
    0 to 1 .... −1
    _____

7. Performance on Behavior Management Treatment Training (BMTT)/Behavior Management System (BMS)
    White status 2
    Pink or green status (level II or III) 0
    Gold status .... −2
    _____

8. Treatment Plan Performance
    In compliance with 0–24% of performance goals 2
    In compliance with 25–49% of performance goals 1
    In compliance with 50–75% of performance goals 0
    In compliance with 76–100% of performance goals .... −1
    _____

                                                                              Total Score _____

III. Custody Assessment (Circle the appropriate level.)

Minimum   0–8 on Items 1–8
Medium   9–13 on Items 1–8
High   14 on Items 1–8

IV. Mandatory Overrides (Circle all that are applicable. Explain below in comments.)

Current superior court case   Institutional predatory offense (rape, sexual/agg. assault)
Pending superior court case   High-profile/Notorious case
Institutional referral to DA

V. Discretionary Override (Circle all that are applicable. Explain below in comments.)

Poor institutional performance   Protective custody
Mental health risk   Exceptional institutional performance
Suicide risk   Medical needs _____
Mental disability

VI. Recommended Custody Level (Circle appropriate level.)

Minimum   Medium   High   Special Management

Signature: _____   Date: ____/____/____ Time: _____a.m./p.m.

VII. Supervisor-Approved Custody Level (Approval required if override indicated. Circle appropriate level.)

Minimum   Medium   High   Special Management

Supervisor Signature: _____   Date: ____/____/____ Time: _____a.m./p.m.

VIII. Comments

Appendix G: Georgia Department of Juvenile Justice Housing Assignment Matrix

I. Identification

Name: _____ DJJ ID#:_____ SSN#:_____

Facility: _____ DOB:_____ Gender: Male / Female

Custody level: Minimum Medium High Sp. Mgmt.   Age: _____ Height: _____ Weight: _____ Size: _____

Date of admission: _____   Current housing type: Initial I II III Special

II. Housing Assessment (Circle the category for each housing criteria that best describes the youth. For example, if the youth's current charge is burglary, circle "Nonpredatory felony.")

Housing Criteria	Type I	Type II	Type III
Current offense	Superior court—Person Person-to-person offense with injury	Nonpredatory felony (weapon, property, drug) or misdemeanor	Status/Traffic offense
Age	18+	13–16	Low through 12
Most serious prior offense	Superior court—Person Person-to-person offense with injury	Nonpredatory felony (weapon, property, drug) or misdemeanor	Status/Traffic offense/None
Most serious prior institutional misconduct during past 12 months	Predatory major disciplinary report	Major—Nonpredatory	Minor/None
Number predatory institutional reports during past 12 months	3+	1–2	0
Sexual behavior	Predatory	Nonpredatory	Victim
Medical	Contagious	No medical problems/Noncontagious	Pregnant

Placement/Housing Matrix

Population	Definition	Housing Decision	Room Selection
Type I	1+ type I category	Single room	Single room
	1+ type I category but 30 days free of major, person-to-person institutional misconduct report	Double room after 30 days	Type I
Type II	Mix of type II or type III categories	Dorm or double room	Type II and type III
Type III	4+ type III categories	Single or double room	Type II or type III

Housing Selection Criteria:

Match Age: Low–12   12–14   14–16   17+
Match Size: Above average—above average or average
              Average—average or below average
              Below average—below average

III. Overrides

Discretionary override, place in a single room.

Pregnant   Mental health
Developmental disability/Delay   Medical

IV. Recommended Housing Category (Circle the appropriate housing category.)

Type I
Type II
Type III

Special housing: _____

JCO:_____

                                                                      Date

Shift commander:

_____

Placement:

_____
                Unit   Room   Bed

Comments:

Appendix H: Juvenile Probation and Aftercare
Sample Risk Assessment Instrument

Select the highest point total applicable for each category:

Score

1. Age at First Adjudication

   16 or older = 0
   14 or 15 = 3
   13 or younger = 5

   _____

2. Prior Criminal Behavior

   No prior arrests = 0
   Prior arrest record, no formal sanctions = 2
   Prior delinquency petitions sustained, no assaultive = 3
   Prior delinquency petitions sustained for assaultive offense = 5

   _____

3. Institutional Commitments or Placements of 30 Days or More

   None = 0
   One = 2
   Two or more = 4

   _____

4. Drug/Chemical Use

   No known use, or no interference with functioning = 0
   Some disruption of functioning = 2
   Chronic abuse or dependency = 5

   _____

5. Alcohol Abuse

   No known use, or no interference with functioning = 0
   Occasional abuse, some disruption of functioning = 1
   Chronic abuse, serious disruption of functioning = 3

   _____

6. Parental Control

   Generally effective = 0
   Inconsistent and/or ineffective = 2
   Little or none = 4

   _____

7. School Disciplinary Problems

   Attending, graduated, or GED = 0
   Problems handled at school level = 1
   Severe truancy or behavioral problems = 3
   Not attending/expelled = 5

   _____

8. Peer Relationships

   Good support and influence = 0
   Negative influence, companions involved in delinquent behavior = 2
   Gang member = 4

   _____

                                                        Total   _____

www.ingramcontent.com/pod-product-compliance
Lightning Source LLC
Chambersburg PA
CBHW080619180526
45168CB00007B/2980